Consider Prayer and Creation

This is an IndieMosh book

brought to you by MoshPit Publishing
an imprint of Mosher's Business Support Pty Ltd

PO Box 4363
Penrith NSW 2750

indiemosh.com.au

A catalogue record for this work is available from the National Library of Australia

https://www.nla.gov.au/collections

Title: Consider Prayer and Creation

Author: Gerber, Deanne Robyn

ISBNs: 9781922628435 (paperback)

Subjects: RELIGION/Biblical meditations/general; RELIGION/devotional; BODY, MIND & SPIRIT/general; NATURE/general

Cover photography by Deanne Gerber. Cover design and layout by Deanne Gerber and Ally Mosher at allymosher.com

Consider Prayer and Creation

Deanne Robyn Gerber

Books written by this author

Consider Job

- *Brain Strainers*
- *Collage*
- *Colouring In*
- *Colour and Draw*
- *Crosswords*
- *Decoder*
- *Figure It Out*
- *Finger Painting*
- *Grids*
- *Little Puppets*
- *Sand Play*
- *Sponge Printing*
- *Stop, Think, Imagine, Express...*
- *True or False?*
- *Who/What Am I?*
- *Wordsearch*
- *Write Your Own Story*

Consider Prayer and Creation

Musicals written by this author

Consider Ezekiel

Consider James

Consider Prayer and Creation
is dedicated to my dear friend Narelle.

Dear Narelle,
Whenever we meet (even if it is many months apart) it is as though we saw each other yesterday. We never seem to grow apart. I thank God for our friendship, a friendship that has lasted more than fifty years.

I want to thank you for the really special times we've had together and pray there will be many more. You are a treasured friend.

May God bless you, dear friend.

CREATION

Awesome

Diverse and Complex

Ordered

Incredible

Points to the Creator God

Dear Awesome Lord,

You created the heavens and the earth. Thank You for showing me a glimpse of Yourself in sweeping beaches, mighty mountains and deep valleys. I am reminded of You when I hear a bird sing or see a butterfly go by. I am reminded of Your presence and gentleness in a soft, barely discernible breeze. I am reminded of Your strength and power when I feel the sun beating down upon me or when I am buffeted by a really strong wind. I am reminded of Your presence when I see sunrays shining brightly around a black cloud. Thank You, dear Awesome Lord, for the beauty and diversity of Your creation.

Amen.

Genesis 1:1; Psalm 33:9; Romans 1:20; Psalm 19:1–4a.

A SPECK OF DUST

Dirty

Unlovely

Barely noticed

A nuisance

Unwanted

Dear Incredible Lord,

You are omniscient and eternal. You are compassionate, gracious, loving, patient and forgiving. Who am I compared to You? I am just a speck of dust.

Yet You love this speck of dust.

You wipe away the tears of this speck of dust before I am swallowed up by the mud I have created by my flood of tears.

All this is beyond my comprehension, but thank You, dear Incredible Lord.

Amen.

Psalm 103:8–14; Genesis 2:7.

RAINBOWS

A rainbow in the clouds

Vibrant

Beautiful

Bands of colour

Arches from one side to another

Dear Faithful Lord,

Thank You for keeping Your promise to Noah and all generations. You are totally trustworthy. Not once have You broken any of Your promises. You have kept them all. You are vibrant, breathtakingly beautiful, gorgeous and glorious. Your world is full of colour. Your love, faithfulness, and abundant and gracious blessings arch from one generation to the next over and over again. Thank You, dear Faithful Lord.

Amen.

Genesis 9:12–17; Joshua 21:45; Psalm 145:13; Psalm 100:5.

COBWEBS

Some are fuzzy
like cotton wool

Some are beautiful
geometric designs

Some look like wool

Dear Wonderful Lord,

You are the Creator and Sustainer of all. I have been made in Your image and yet I stuff cotton wool in my ears so I can't hear You. I let the world, Satan and my sinful desires pull the wool over my eyes. Please unstop my ears so I can hear You. Please open my eyes so I might see clearly. Please forgive me and lift me up. Thank You, dear Wonderful Lord.

Amen.

Genesis 1:26–28; Mark 7:34–37; Mark 10:52; James 4:4–10; 1 Peter 5:6–11.

STONES

Hard

Inflict pain

Rough

Jagged edges

Unyielding

Dear Omniscient Lord,

You see everything, including my sin and hardness of heart. I am so sorry for the pain I cause You. I am so sorry for the pain I cause others. I am truly sorry for my sins. Help me to resist sin and yield to Your will. Please soften my heart. Please smooth my jagged edges, dear Omniscient Lord.

Amen.

Ezekiel 18:30; Romans 6:12–14; Ezekiel 36:26, 27.

SEEDS

Small

Insignificant

Perishable

Limited lifespan

Dried up

Dear Eternal Lord,

You are God and Your ways are truly amazing, but I am so small and insignificant. You are eternal but I have a limited lifespan. You don't age, shrivel, dry up or die but I will age, shrivel, dry up and die. Thank You that through Your enduring Word, I can be born again of imperishable seed. Thank You for Your kingdom, dear Eternal Lord.

Amen.

Isaiah 55:9; Psalm 93:2; 1 Peter 1:23; Daniel 4:3; Matthew 13:31, 32.

TREES

One solitary blossom on a very dead-looking tree.

In vain, I examined a streetful of trees for more blossoms
but there were none.

Day after day I looked and still none.

Then one day I noticed that the solitary tiny, delicate and
pink blossom I had first espied had died.

Once again the landscape was one of
lifeless tree after lifeless tree.

*Sometime later, there were trees covered with
tiny, delicate pink blossoms.*

*This made me think of Jesus dying and rising from the dead
so we could have life.*

Dear Living Lord,

Thank You for sending Jesus so my sins can be forgiven. Thank You for raising Jesus back to life and seating Him at Your right hand. Jesus is King of kings and Lord of lords. May He be King and Lord of my life. One day Jesus will return. Thank You, dear Living Lord!

Amen.

Romans 8:34; Revelation 17:14; Acts 1:11; Revelation 1:5–7.

MOTHS

Powdery

Senseless

Eat holes in clothes

Undesirable

Die in the light

Dear Gracious Lord,

Moths remind me that I need to store up for myself moth-safe and rust-free treasures in heaven and not treasures on earth. I am senseless, and undesirable sin eats away at me. However, because of Jesus, I won't die in Your glorious light! Thank You so much, dear Gracious Lord.

Amen.

Matthew 6:19–21; Jude 24, 25.

CLOUDS

Scattered

Fluffy

Different hues

*Make sunrises and sunsets
more spectacular*

Dear Magnificent Lord,

Grey clouds make me see myself as I truly am—full of sin, scatty and scattered. Please forgive all my sins.

Romans 3:10–18; 1 John 1:8.

White clouds make me see myself as You do—cleansed and made pure by Jesus. Thank You, dearest Lord.

Isaiah 1:18; 1 Corinthians 6:11.

Clouds of different hues make me see myself as others do. You use what is dirty and stained to reflect Your glory and light. Might You be glorified, dear Magnificent Lord.

Amen.

2 Corinthians 3:18; Matthew 5:14–16.

RAIN

Raindrops on a leaf

Puddles of water

Water sinking into the dry earth

New life

Plants flowering

Dear Life-giving Lord,

Rain is a wonderful gift from You. An even more wonderful gift from You is Jesus and the gift of eternal life. Thank You for the Holy Spirit. I am being renewed day by day. Thank You, dear Life-giving Lord.

Amen.

Deuteronomy 11:13–15; John 3:16; Titus 3:5–7; 2 Corinthians 4:16.

WIND

Leaves being tossed by the wind

The wind kissing my face

Fresh

Invigorating

Strong

Dear Invisible Lord,

The wind reminds me that even though You are unseen, You are there. It obeys You and accomplishes what You want it to do. The wind is a wonderful reminder that You are both powerful and gentle. You refresh my soul. Thank You, dear Invisible Lord.

Amen.

1 Timothy 1:17; Exodus 14:21, 22; Mark 4:35-41; Matthew 11:29; Psalm 23:3.

PALM TREES

Tall

Straight

Shaggy

Palm branches

No foothold

Dear Blessed Lord,

Palm trees remind me that a great crowd praised Jesus as king. Palm trees also remind me of the great multitude in heaven. Help me not to give Satan a foothold in my life. Please remove my shagginess and make my path straight, dear Blessed Lord.

Amen.

John 12:12–15; Revelation 7:9–17; Ephesians 6:10–18; James 4:7; Proverbs 3:5, 6.

LILIES

White

Velvety

Smooth

Unblemished

Fit for a bride

Dear Holy Lord,

You are holy, pure, gentle and full of love. Please cleanse me so I don't gratify the desires of my sinful nature. Please clothe me with Jesus. Help me to be holy as You are holy, dear Holy Lord.

Amen.

Romans 13:14; 1 Peter 1:13–16.

DROUGHT

Parched

Cracked

Dry

Brown

No sign of life

Dear Reviving Lord,

Wherever I turn, all I can see is a parched, dry and cracked land. Sometimes my life seems like this. You and only You can revive me. You and only You can quench my thirst. Please refresh me. Please fill me with Your Spirit, dear Reviving Lord.

Amen.

Psalm 143:6; Isaiah 43:19–21; John 7:37, 38; Isaiah 32:15.

FOG

Opaque

Eerie

Heavy

Like a blanket

Clinging

Dear Caring Lord,

I watch the fog lifting in the morning and underneath I can see still, clear water. It reminds me of when You lift my sins and anxious thoughts and underneath, I feel calm and at peace. Thank You that I can pray to You about anything at any time of the day or night. Thank You for caring. Thank You for Your wonderful peace, dear Caring Lord.

Amen.

Isaiah 44:22; 1 Peter 5:7; Philippians 4:6–8.

FRAGRANT FLOWERS

Heady

Attractive

Sweet

Intoxicating

Enticing

Dear Sweet Lord,

Thank You that You sent Your one and only Son, Jesus, whom You loved dearly, to die for me. I am truly grateful for this sweet, sweet sacrifice. Just as fragrant flowers give off a beautiful perfume might I, dear Sweet Lord, give off a beautiful perfume to attract others to You.

Amen.

Ephesians 5:1, 2; 2 Corinthians 2:14, 15.

FRUIT

Luscious

Full of flavour

Nutritious

Attached to the branch

Essential

Dear Amazing Lord,

You are the gardener—Jesus is the vine and I am a branch. Please help me remain in Him. Help me to produce good fruit. May the fruit of the Spirit be evident in my life. Please draw others to Yourself, dear Amazing Lord, so that they too can taste and see that You are good.

Amen.

John 15:1-8; Galatians 5:22, 23; Psalm 34:8.

SAND

Fresh

Windblown

Soft

Soothing

Smooth

One morning I went to a quiet beach and prayed. There were lots of holes in the sand. As I looked at the sand in front of me I saw two black eyes looking out of a hole.

The next day I looked for my little friend but there was no sign of him anywhere—just sand as far as the eye could see. Not a hole in sight.

Suddenly something popped out of the sand. Like a chick hatching from an egg, a crab broke its way through the flat, unbroken surface. He stayed half-in and half-out of his hole. What was he doing? Was he having a sunbake? Was he resting? After a while, he scooped out some more sand, then some more, then stopped for a while. This continued—scooping, scooping and a short rest.

I saw another crab doing the same but he wasn't working as hard as the first crab. Then my little friend just disappeared.

As I left, I went over and looked closely at my little friend's hole. It was so deep I couldn't see the bottom of the tunnel. No wonder he'd needed to rest!

Dear Loving Lord,

Thank You for the joy I experienced from observing the antics of one of Your little creatures. Thank You that Jesus broke into our world. Thank You for Your deep, deep love. You fill the hole in my life. I know You observe all my antics and You see whether I work wholeheartedly or half-heartedly. Please forgive my apathy and please help me to serve You joyfully and wholeheartedly. May I one day enter Your rest, dear Loving Lord.

Amen.

Luke 2:10–14; Romans 8:39; Psalm 139:1–18; Revelation 3:16; Hebrews 4:9–11.

BIRDS

Graceful

Soaring

Carefree

Unhurried

Travelling together

Dear Dependable Lord,

A flock of birds flies across the sky, reminding me that You will carry, protect and provide for me. Thank You for Your wonderful care of me. Thank You for Your faithfulness. Thank You that I can feel safe in You, dear Dependable Lord.

Amen.

Exodus 19:4; Psalm 91:1-4; Matthew 6:26, 27; 2 Samuel 22:2, 3.

SUN

Glorious

Beautiful

Warm

Sheds light far and wide

Incredible reflections

Dear Glorious Lord,

Thank You for showing me a glimpse of Your glory and majesty once again in a magnificent sunset. The sunset was beautiful, as You are beautiful. It thrilled my heart and made me gasp, so great was the wonder of its beauty. Your beauty, glory, splendour, power and majesty take my breath away. Thank You, dear Glorious Lord, for who You are and all You do.

Amen.

1 Chronicles 29:11; Revelation chapter 4.

ABOUT THE AUTHOR

Australian author Deanne Robyn Gerber loves God and the work He gives her to do. Married with 4 adult children and 12 surviving grandchildren, Deanne initially qualified in Early Childhood Education and has completed studies at Moore Theological College and Sydney Missionary and Bible College. Deanne loves going for a walk each day. As she walks she looks at her surroundings. Often she prays as she walks. Sometimes she takes photos. Sometimes she "stops and smells the roses". *Consider Prayer and Creation* is the result of these cherished and refreshing times.

Lightning Source UK Ltd.
Milton Keynes UK
UKHW050224080721
386806UK00002B/51